Human Body Systems

The Endocrine System

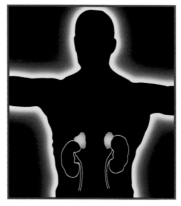

by Rebecca Olien

Consultant:
Marjorie Hogan, MD
Pediatrician
Hennepin County Medical Center
Minneapolis, Minnesota

Capstone
press

Mankato, Minnesota

Bridgestone Books are published by Capstone Press,
151 Good Counsel Drive, P.O. Box 669, Mankato, Minnesota 56002.
www.capstonepress.com

Library of Congress Cataloging-in-Publication Data
Olien, Rebecca.
   The endocrine system / by Rebecca Olien.
      p. cm.—(Bridgestone books. Human body systems)
      Summary: "Learn about the job of the endocrine system, problems that may arise, and how to keep
the body system healthy"—Provided by publisher.
      Includes bibliographical references and index.
      ISBN-13: 978-0-7368-5410-8 (hardcover)
      ISBN-10: 0-7368-5410-X (hardcover)
      1. Endocrine glands—Juvenile literature. I. Title. II. Bridgestone books. Human body systems.
QP187.O545 2006
612.4—dc22   2005021150

Editorial Credits
Amber Bannerman, editor; Bobbi J. Dey, designer; Kelly Garvin, photo researcher/photo editor;
   Tami Collins and Scott Thoms, illustrators

Photo Credits
Capstone Press/Karon Dubke, cover (girl)
Corbis/Ariel Skelley, 20; Jose Luis Pelaez Inc., 4; Karen Kasmauski, 18; Michael Freeman, 14; Star, 10
Peter Arnold Inc./Alex Grey, 16
Photo Researchers Inc./Alfred Pasieka/Science Photo Library, cover (glands), 1, 6; Anatomical
   Travelogue, 12

1 2 3 4 5 6 11 10 09 08 07 06

Table of Contents

Growing

How much have you grown since last year? Maybe you have grown a couple of inches and gained a few pounds. Your endocrine system helps you grow taller and bigger. It also tells your body to cry when you are sad and to scream when you are scared.

Your body is made of many systems that all work together. They help you do things like paint, brush your hair, and play with your pets. When your dog or cat scratches your arm, your systems help you say, "Ouch!"

◄ When you go to the doctor's office, someone checks your height to see how much you've grown.

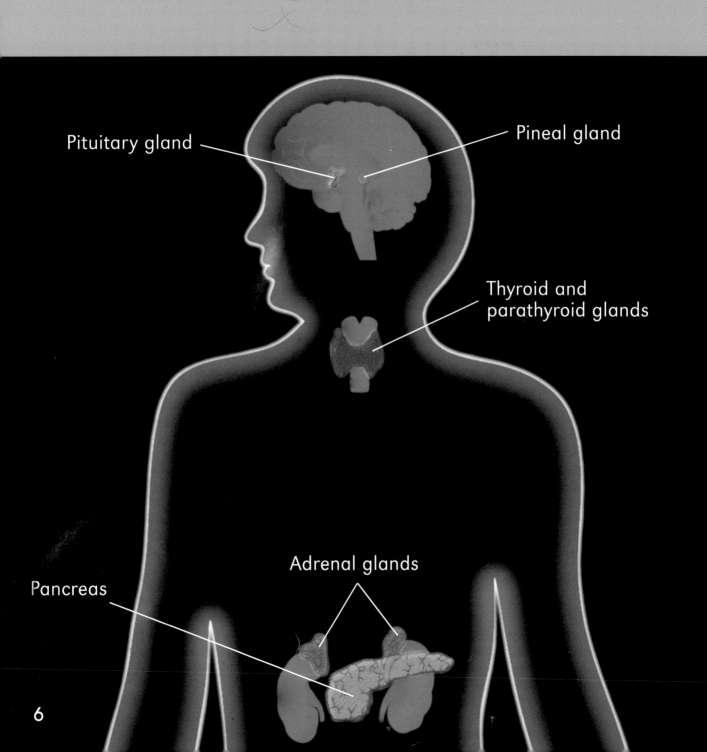

Pituitary gland

Pineal gland

Thyroid and
parathyroid glands

Adrenal glands

Pancreas

Glands

Glands are small organs in your body. Your pituitary and pineal glands are in your brain. Thyroid and parathyroid glands are in your neck. Your adrenal glands and pancreas are found just below your stomach.

Your glands make chemicals called **hormones**. Hormones send signals throughout the body. At any time, at least 30 hormones are flowing through your body. Scientists keep finding new hormones all the time.

◀ Glands send hormones into the blood.

Traveling Hormones

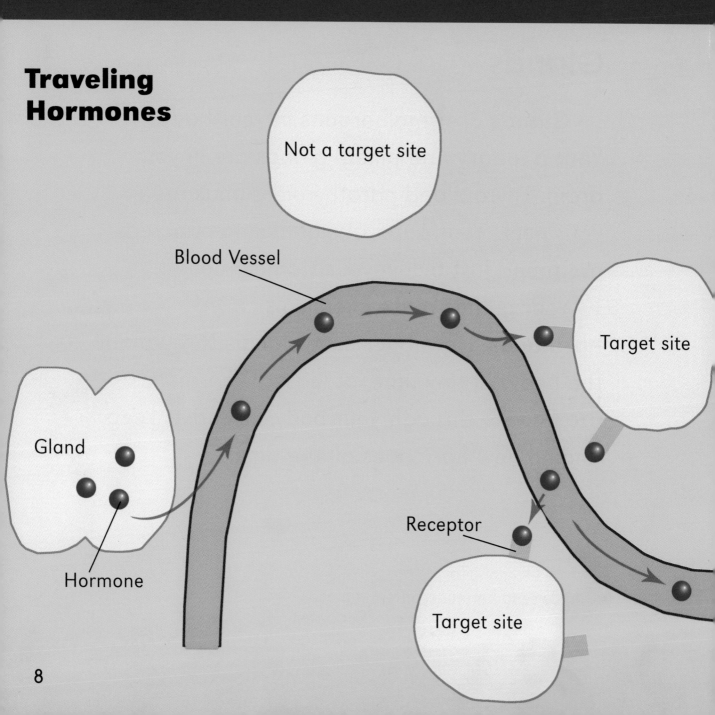

Not a target site

Blood Vessel

Target site

Gland

Hormone

Receptor

Target site

How Hormones Work

Hormones deliver messages to certain body **cells**, called target sites. Blood helps hormones travel to where they need to go.

Target sites use **receptors** to pick up certain hormones. Hormones then tell body parts and cells what to do. When you exercise, hormones that make you feel good are released.

◀ Hormones travel from glands through the blood to target sites.

Glands in the Brain

The most important gland in the body is only the size of a pea. It is the pituitary gland found in your brain. The brain's hypothalamus and the pituitary gland work together to release hormones that control other glands. The pituitary gland sends hormones to help you grow, develop, and feel good.

The pineal gland is also in the brain. It makes a hormone that controls how much we sleep. Light changes the amount of the hormone our pineal gland makes. We often sleep more during the short days of winter.

◄ Your pineal gland controls how long you sleep.

Thyroid Gland

Parathyroid Glands

Glands in the Neck

The thyroid gland is a butterfly-shaped gland in the lower neck. It makes hormones that control how the body uses energy. Greater amounts of the thyroid hormone increase **metabolism**. If you eat a lot but don't gain weight easily, you probably have a high metabolism.

Four small parathyroid glands are connected to the thyroid gland. These glands produce hormones that control calcium in the body. Calcium helps bones grow and stay strong.

◄ The four small parathyroid glands are found on the back of the thyroid gland.

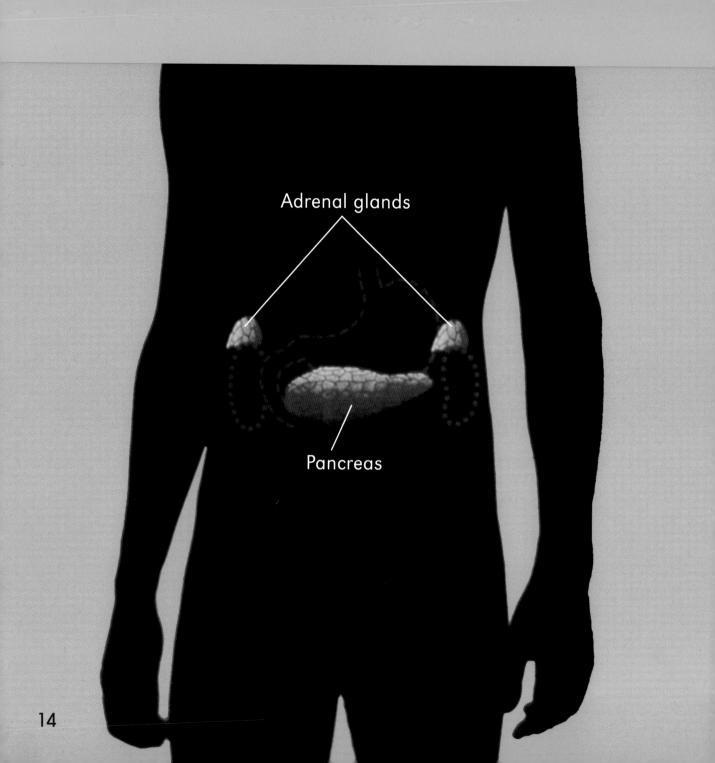

Adrenal glands

Pancreas

Adrenal Glands and Pancreas

Adrenal glands send out a hormone called **adrenaline**. Adrenaline makes your heart beat faster and makes sugar pour into your blood. Imagine walking through your house, when suddenly your little brother or sister jumps out and says, "Boo!" You scream, all with the help of adrenaline.

After an adrenaline rush, your body needs to even out the sugar in your blood. The pancreas makes the **insulin** hormone to control the sugar in your blood.

◄ The pancreas is a major organ and a gland found below the stomach. Your adrenal glands rest on top of your kidneys.

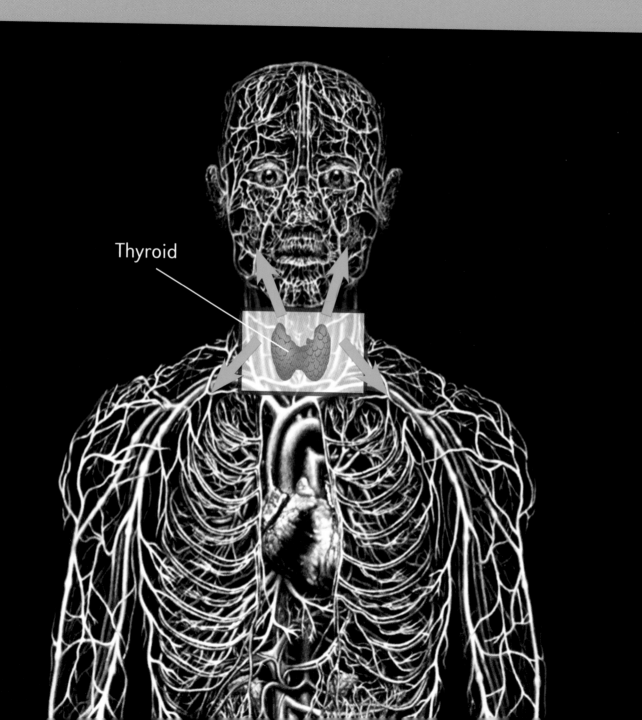

Thyroid

Systems Work Together

The endocrine system works with the circulatory system to deliver hormones. Your strong heart and blood vessels make up your circulatory system. Your heart pumps blood through your bloodstream.

Glands send hormones into your bloodstream. Hormones are able to reach all parts of the body through the blood.

◀ The thyroid gland sends hormones throughout the body on a pathway of blood vessels.

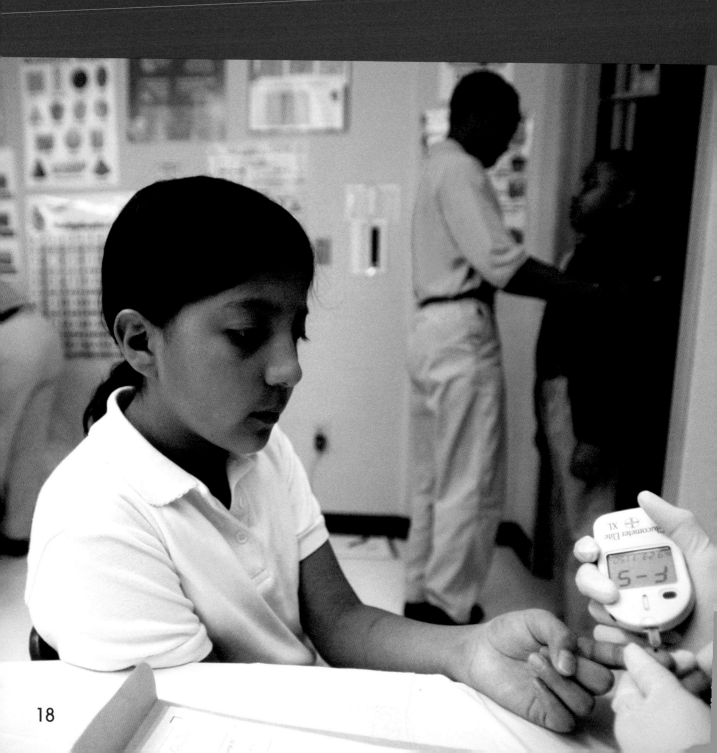

Endocrine Problems

The endocrine system needs to make just the right amount of each hormone. Too little or too much of a hormone can make you sick.

Diabetes is a common health problem caused by too little of the insulin hormone. Insulin helps the body use sugar. When a person has diabetes, his or her cells don't use insulin properly. Sugar stays in the blood. Too much blood sugar makes the body sick. People with diabetes can take insulin to help their cells use sugar correctly.

◀ A patient gets her blood tested to check sugar levels.

Keeping Healthy

Eating healthy foods helps the endocrine system. The body needs vitamins, protein, minerals, and other nutrients to function properly. Eating too much fat or sugar can cause weight gain. Being too heavy can lead to diabetes and other endocrine problems.

Exercise helps blood move and organs work. Exercise also makes the heart stronger. A strong heart helps carry hormones in the blood. All body systems work better when you exercise and eat right.

◄ Eating healthy food gives your body needed nutrients.

Glossary

adrenaline (uh-DREN-uh-lin)—a substance released by the adrenal glands when a person gets scared or excited

cell (SEL)—a tiny part of the body; cells make up body parts.

diabetes (dye-uh-BEE-teez)—a disease in which there is too much sugar in the blood

gland (GLAND)—a small organ in your body that makes chemicals called hormones

hormone (HOR-mohn)—one of several chemical messengers that control the organs of the body

insulin (IN-suh-luhn)—a hormone made in the pancreas that controls the amount of sugar in the blood

metabolism (muh-TAB-uh-liz-uhm)—how the body changes food into energy

receptor (ri-SEP-tuhr)—the part of a cell that receives information; receptors on cells pick up certain hormones.

Read More

Carter, Alden R. *I'm Tougher than Diabetes!* Morton Grove, Ill.: A. Whitman and Co., 2001.

Parker, Steve. *Hormones.* Body Focus. Chicago: Heinemann, 2003.

Internet Sites

FactHound offers a safe, fun way to find Internet sites related to this book. All of the sites on FactHound have been researched by our staff.

Here's how:

1. Visit *www.facthound.com*
2. Type in this special code **073685410X** for age-appropriate sites. Or enter a search word related to this book for a more general search.
3. Click on the **Fetch It** button.

FactHound will fetch the best sites for you!

Index